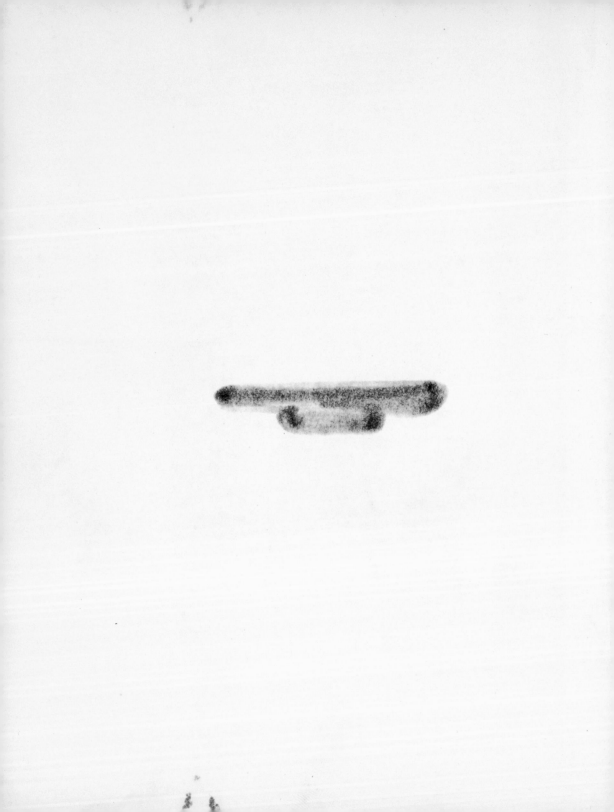

# SHAYS' REBELLION

"In 1786-87 the farmer-veterans of the American Revolution took up arms again in Massachusetts, where the Revolution had begun, in order to protest laws in their state that made a mockery of their sacrifices for freedom. They were outraged at legislation, and particularly taxation, that discriminated against the hard-pressed laborers and favored the property-owners who had stayed at home during the war for freedom from tyranny and unjust taxation."

## PRINCIPALS

DANIEL SHAYS, leader of the rebellion; the Revolutionary War captain who would not endure unjust legislation in the new nation he had fought to establish.

JAMES BOWDOIN, governor of Massachusetts, who called out the state militia to subdue the rebels.

GENERAL BENJAMIN LINCOLN, who led the militia to rout the rebels at Petersham, Massachusetts, on February 4, 1787.

LUKE DAY, a veteran officer of the Revolution, whom the Bible inspired to rouse poor farmers like himself against the lawcourts that were sentencing them to jail for debt.

ARTEMAS WARD, first commander of the patriot forces in the Revolution and later a judge who risked his life to uphold law and order in Massachusetts.

Daniel Shays (1747-1825). This, the only
known portrait of the leader of Shays' Rebellion, was probably not drawn from life.

A FOCUS BOOK

# Shays' Rebellion
## 1786-7

*Americans Take Up Arms Against Unjust Laws*

by Monroe Stearns

Illustrated with photographs and contemporary prints

FRANKLIN WATTS, INC.

575 Lexington Avenue　　　New York, N.Y. 10022

*The authors and publishers of the Focus Books wish to acknowledge the helpful editorial suggestions of Professor Richard B. Morris.*

Cover photo: Artemas Ward defying the rebellious farmers on the steps of the Worcester Court House, a drawing by Howard Pyle.

SBN 531-01003-1

Copyright © 1968 by Franklin Watts, Inc.
Library of Congress Catalog Card Number: 68-17705
Printed in the United States of America
2   3   4   5

# Contents

Greenwood 5/22/70 2.44

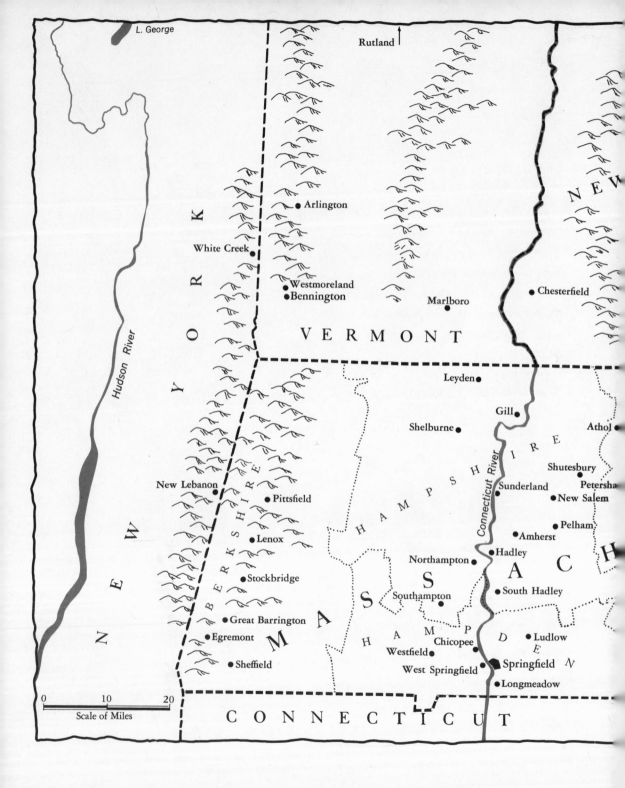

L. George

Rutland↑

NEW

Hudson River

YORK

Arlington

White Creek

Westmoreland
Bennington

Marlboro

Chesterfield

VERMONT

Leyden

Gill

Athol

Shelburne

HAMPSHIRE

Shutesbury

New Lebanon

BERKSHIRE

Pittsfield

Sunderland

Petersha

New Salem

Lenox

Pelham

Connecticut River

Amherst

Hadley

Stockbridge

Northampton

South Hadley

MASSACH

Southampton

Great Barrington

HAMP

Egremont

Chicopee

Ludlow

Westfield

D

E

Sheffield

West Springfield

Springfield

N

Longmeadow

NEW

0        10        20
Scale of Miles

CONNECTICUT

The region of Shays' Rebellion.

# Daniel Shays Fights for Freedom

On the morning of April 20, 1775, the day after the battles of Lexington and Concord had begun the American Revolution, Daniel Shays marched off with the other minutemen of Brookfield, Massachusetts, to join the patriot army which was gathering in Cambridge.

Shays was only an ensign under Rufus Putnam, the captain of the Brookfield militia. After he fought at the Battle of Bunker Hill, on June 17, 1775, however, he was commended for bravery and promoted to sergeant.

Many of the men who had joined the poorly organized and poorly equipped American Army against the British went home after the period of their enlistment was over, but Daniel Shays stayed on. He dreamed of a glorious future for himself as a soldier for liberty. Certainly there would be no glory for him as a hired farmhand.

For all of his twenty-eight years Daniel Shays had been poor, and his father, Patrick, had been poor before him. Patrick Shays (or Shea, or Shay — the spelling of proper names was far from uniform before the census of 1790 tended to standardize it) had emigrated from Ireland as an indentured servant; that is, as soon as he arrived in Massachusetts, his services were sold at auction to a farmer of Hopkinton, who paid the shipowner for young Patrick's passage to America. The lad was then bound to work for this farmer without pay until his labor had earned back the auction price.

In 1744, Patrick married an Irish girl named Margaret Dempsey. Three years later, Daniel was born to them, probably after his sister.

The family was too poor for the boy to get any education beyond the three R's, which he could learn at the free school of Hopkinton, a town of about one thousand inhabitants. As soon as Daniel was old enough to earn his own living, he hired out to a farmer in Framingham, then moved to a better job in the western frontier town of Great

Barrington. He was short and strong, and a good worker, and he was ambitious. When he saw another chance to improve himself, he moved eastward to Brookfield, where he was able to earn $53 a year — a little more than the going wage. There, in 1773, he married Abigail, daughter of Jonathan Gilbert, Brookfield's leading citizen.

Daniel Shays yearned to free himself from the backbreaking, dawn-to-dusk toil of a farmer. Even if he had owned his own farm, he would barely have made a living from it. The average farm in New England at that time was seventy acres, of which only seven were cultivable. A farmer did well to support his family on its produce. He might get fifty dollars a year in cash from the sale of surplus or from the wooden utensils, called treen, which he could make during the winters.

Shays saw himself, and all farmers like him, as essential to society as a whole, but as neglected members of that society. His sense of neglect made him scornful of the standards and customs of those who ignored him. He grew independent. He wanted recognition.

Daniel loved to talk, and he talked well. Other men liked him. In the taverns, he was loud in support of those who clamored for freedom from British oppression. To their arguments he added his own for equality. What would liberty mean if the rich merchants of the seacoast continued to dominate the Massachusetts legislature, known as the General Court, at the expense of the poor farmers and their rights?

The Army had already given Daniel Shays a promotion. It was a citizens' army; preferment did not have to be bought, it could be earned. There was no telling how high a man like Daniel Shays, eager to fight for freedom and equality, might rise in it.

By 1776, Shays was a lieutenant in a regiment defending New England's western frontier against any invasion that might come from British Canada. Often he was sent on recruiting expeditions; he more than filled his quota of enlistments in the Army. Finally he persuaded

[4]

a batch of recruits to elect him their captain — a common custom in the militia — and when he brought them in, he insisted on being commissioned a captain in the Continental Army.

Shays' demand horrified the Army officers, but Daniel stuck to it — no captaincy, no men. The Army was desperate for soldiers. Shays won his point. He was promised his commission. He did not get it, however, until 1779, when he won it with pay retroactive to January, 1778.

Meanwhile Shays had fought at Ticonderoga, and at Saratoga, and perhaps at Bennington. In one of those engagements he was wounded. For the rest of his life he carried the scar of a saber cut on his cheek.

In 1778, while on military duty in Albany, New York, Shays joined the Freemasons. Brigadier General John Stark, the victor at the important Battle of Bennington, may even have sponsored him for membership in his lodge. They had fought together at Bunker Hill. Daniel Shays was ever a sensible, attractive fellow, with a gallant style about him.

Daniel was coming up in the world socially, but not financially. In February, 1779, his wife wrote him that she had had to borrow four hundred dollars from his friend William Conkey, the tavern keeper of Pelham, Massachusetts, for whom Daniel had done several favors. Daniel's finances made a turn for the better, however, when, after fighting under Anthony Wayne and Rufus Putnam in the capture of the fort at Stony Point, New York, on July 15, 1779, the captain got a share of the booty. He needed every penny he could get from selling it. Neither men nor officers were paid regularly by the Continental Congress. Even when they were, the pay was in paper dollars, and the dollar in those days was worth about twenty-five cents, and was rapidly going down in value. It would cost a year of a captain's pay to buy a pair of shoes or a good meal.

Later in 1779, Shays was transferred to the regiment commanded

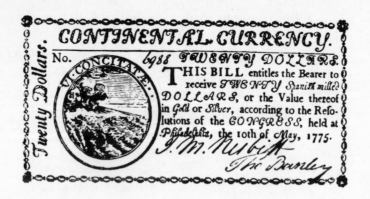

This $20 bill issued by the Continental Congress in 1775 is an example of the practically worthless paper money with which the veterans of the Revolution were paid. It was not accepted as payment for debts or taxes.

by Rufus Putnam, then a colonel, in Newark, New Jersey.

On May 10, 1780, the Marquis de Lafayette, who had aided the Americans since 1777, returned to Morristown, New Jersey, from a visit to his native France. He brought with him several handsome swords which he proceeded to give to distinguished American Army officers. One went to Captain Daniel Shays for his conspicuous bravery, his efficiency, and his thoughtful treatment of his men.

Shays already had a sword that had served him well. What he did not have was money, either for his own needs or those of his wife and two sons, Daniel, Jr., and Hiram. He sold the sword Lafayette had presented to him.

Shays' action scandalized his fellow officers. They talked of court-martialing him for conduct unbecoming to an officer and a gentleman.

Suddenly the popular, the proud, Captain Shays found himself shunned and shamed. What hurt him even more than this ostracism was his discovery that the Army he had thought so democratic had become class-conscious.

The morale of the Army was extremely low. Enlistments had fallen off. There were scores of desertions. There were mutinies. A crisis over the officers' pay caused many of them to resign in October, 1780.

Daniel Shays was one of those. Utterly disillusioned, he went home to Brookfield.

# Distress and Disappointment

On October 25, 1780, rich John Hancock of Boston took office as the first governor of the Commonwealth of Massachusetts under its new state constitution. This instrument of government provided for a legislature of two chambers, to which the people could elect representatives who had sufficient property to qualify.

Daniel Shays immediately distrusted these property qualifications. They would give too much control to the rich merchants of the sea-coast, and too little to the poor farmers of the interior. He knew from having lived in some of the towns in the western part of the state that not all of them had a man rich enough to qualify for the House of Representatives, much less for the upper chamber, the Senate.

Brookfield was too near the prosperous eastern towns for these opinions of Shays' to be popular. In addition, his prominent father-in-law criticized him severely for having sold Lafayette's gift and for having resigned his commission. It appeared to Daniel Shays that there were rich men who had stayed in their warm, comfortable houses while the soldiers were starving and freezing at Valley Forge and

Morristown, and that he and his comrades had one view of the liberty they were fighting for, while those rich men had another, quite different view. It occurred to Shays that all the farmer-soldiers might be winning was economic stability for the merchants who had come to them for aid against Britain's taxation and restrictions on commerce. If the war turned out in the patriots' favor, the farmers, Shays thought, should use the peace to get political control of the land they had bled for.

Resentfully Shays pulled up stakes and moved northwest to Pelham, where his friend William Conkey lived. He settled on a small farm on the west branch of the Swift River, in the section of Pelham known as Prescott. (That part of the town is now covered by the waters of the Quabbin Reservoir.) Daniel and Abigail Shays joined the Second Parish Church.

Sociable Daniel won the respect and admiration of his new neighbors. He was elected to the town's Committee of Safety, and he drilled its militia for the defense of Pelham. Since the war was not yet over, a raid by the British was not unlikely. He was also elected one of the town wardens. Best of all, so far as Daniel Shays' pride was concerned, he was considered a gentleman — a term then reserved for educated, professional men.

There was great distress at that time in the rural areas of western Massachusetts. The principal cause was the taxes the legislature was levying in order to pay the interest on the state debt, which was enormous as a result of the staggering costs of the war for independence.

The taxes had to be paid in hard money; that is, actual coin. But there was precious little hard money in the country, for most of it was being drained off to Europe to pay for supplies needed in the war. The farmers had the least cash of all, and they needed all they could lay their hands on for necessities they could not produce themselves.

There were also the debts almost every western farmer owed to some merchant. The eastern merchants were as much in the loan busi-

The home of Daniel Shays in the Prescott section of Pelham, Massachusetts, from a photograph taken about 1900.

ness as in trade. They had loaned the farmers money to buy land, or increase their acreage, or to get livestock and tools. Since sound currency had become almost extinct, these outstanding loans became burdensome to both debtor and creditor, for the merchant creditors demanded interest and principal in hard money. The merchants had seen to it that no law obliged them to accept paper money or goods in payment of a debt.

The merchant creditors brought suits to collect their loans. The indebted farmers had to pay the high cost of these suits before the Court of Common Pleas and of appeals from that court's decision to

The Town Hall of Pelham, Massachusetts, built in 1743. Here about one half of Shays' men camped from January 28 to February 2, 1787; the remainder moved on with Shays to Conkey's Tavern and camped on East Hill.

the Supreme Judicial Court. It was a fearful situation for the debt-ridden farmers, for a judgment against a debtor meant that all his property except his tools and the clothes on his back could be seized and sold — usually at about 20 per cent of its value — to satisfy a creditor's claim.

If the claim could not be satisfied, the debtor could be sentenced to jail and his creditor paid the cost of his board there — about a dollar a week — as long as he wished or until the debtor paid his debt or it was paid for him by his family or friends.

The jails were crowded, ill-ventilated, and filthy. Upright but insolvent farmers were confined with thieves and murderers. These

A facsimile of Daniel Shays' handwriting, with his signature. Like most men of his time, Shays was a poor speller. The note reads: "Pelham November 28 1780 Mr. hunt Plese to Let mr Conke[y] have one Quarter of a pouned of Shuger and Charg the Count [account] to me and and you will [oblige] your Humbbule Sarte [servant] Daniel Shays."

criminals could get bail, but debtors could not. And, of course, a man could also be jailed as a debtor for inability to pay his taxes.

Angry town meetings sent firm instructions to their representatives in the General Court in faraway Boston to have the courts suspend judgments on debtors until more hard money was available. Also they were instructed either to make personal property a legal satisfaction of a claim, or to issue paper money and make it legally acceptable for payment of debts and taxes.

By October, 1781, all relief measures for the poor and the debt-ridden had failed in the General Court. The merchants who dominated the court had no use for the paper money already in existence, and not the slightest wish to issue more.

Except for mopping-up operations, principally in the South, the War for Independence came to an end on October 19, 1781. On that warm, sunny afternoon in Yorktown, Virginia, General Benjamin Lincoln of Hingham, Massachusetts, accepted the British sword of surrender for the American Commander in Chief George Washington.

The returning veterans found the indifference of the General Court a blow to their feelings as well as to their pockets. They felt entitled to retirement and rest. Their souls were heavy with the thought that they had shed their blood on the battlefields only to be worn out with burdensome taxes at home. Had they fought for liberty only to give their creditors the right to drag them into courts that were sending them to jail?

In their disillusionment with the system of government that had been set up during their absence, the veterans revived the institution of the county convention. This was made up of delegates from various town meetings within a county. It served as an outlet for the veterans' feelings and as an expression of their rights. The new state constitution had made the county conventions of doubtful legality, but the town meetings of Hampshire County* called one such convention to meet in Hadley on February 11, 1782.

Daniel Shays was a willing delegate from Pelham. He had recently seen a sick widow's few possessions, including her bed and bedding, sold to satisfy a debt. He was an angry man.

The Hadley convention listed the new taxes and the court judgments on hapless debtors as the chief grievances of the people. It asked the General Court to restore paper money as legal tender, and to accept work on roads as tax payments. It reminded the urban repre-

* Hampshire County then included the present Franklin and Hampden counties. Hampshire was the largest county in Massachusetts — so large, in fact, that it had two county seats, Northampton and Springfield.

sentatives of the more recent settlers' hardships in taming "this howling and frightful wilderness." It complained that even the older towns of the region "groaned under their burden." It got no response whatever from the General Court.

Preacher Samuel Cullick Ely, of the Sunderland congregation, had been one of the loudest promoters of this revival of the county convention to consolidate the desires of a whole district. He, too, was a veteran, as was almost every man of his parish. He blasted the courts; he blasted the merchants who controlled the General Court; he blasted the Massachusetts constitution. "I have in my pocket," he declared, "a constitution that the Angel Gabriel could not find fault with." He called for less talk and more action.

On April 4, 1782, Ely harangued the distressed farmers in Northampton: they should band together and return the following week to prevent the judges from holding court and condemning more debtors.

Closing the courts had been a means of protecting the rebellious colonists from recriminations from the British. Ely cited these precedents as justification for his own rebellious activities.

On April 12, the farmers collected in Northampton to keep the judges from sitting.

"Come on, my brave boys!" Ely shouted to them. "We will go to the woodpile and get clubs enough, and knock their gray wigs off, and send them out of the world in an instant."

Luke Day of West Springfield had been a captain and a brevet major in the Continental Army, and had fought seven years for freedom. Now he was a poor farmer again, but still a law-abiding one. Perhaps he had come to Northampton that April 12 to answer a claim for a debt.

When Day saw Ely's gang marching with bludgeons from the woodpile, he persuaded four fellow veterans to help him oppose them. The five former soldiers spread out across the top of the courthouse steps to protect the judges. The courts sat.

[13]

Sheriff Elisha Porter arrested Ely for disturbing the peace and interfering with justice. The judges whom Ely had hoped to silence sentenced him to jail in Sprinfigeld.

On the morning of June 13, some 120 of Ely's friends and followers started down to Springfield to free their champion. Most of the Springfield men, they knew, would be in nearby Longmeadow that day at a funeral. It was easy for the band to liberate Ely and start north with him.

Hastily Sheriff Porter rallied fifty militiamen and caught up with the rescuers. In the scuffle Ely escaped and disappeared into Vermont, then an independent republic.

# The Tears of the Oppressed

The General Court was advised to deal quickly with the troublesome situation in Hampshire County, which Samuel Ely and his followers had turned into an actual insurrection. The legislature sent a committee of three skillful politicians to reason with the insurgents.

This committee wisely let the angry farmers talk themselves out. Then the politicians persuaded them to remain loyal to the government in spite of their grievances.

Conditions in western Massachusetts, however, did not miraculously improve as a result of the General Court's gesture of interest in the situation. The courts were still ordering the sale of a farmer's goods to satisfy his creditors.

In May, 1783, on the last day of the terms of the Court of Common Pleas (civil) and the Court of General Sessions (criminal) in Springfield, sixty men met in a tavern and declared themselves a convention. They resolved to close the courts before judgments were handed down.

[14]

An early-nineteenth-century view of Court Square, Springfield, Massachusetts, showing the elm tree (center) under which the farmers gathered to oppose the courts in 1783. The old courthouse (now replaced) is shown to the right of the Congregational Church, still standing. Main Street is in the foreground.

When the courthouse bell rang to announce that the judges were approaching to deliver judgments, the "convention," now armed with stout hickory sticks, adjourned to the elm tree a few yards south of the courthouse and blocked the path of the judges as Sheriff Porter ceremoniously escorted them along Main Street.

Sheriff Porter appealed to the inhabitants of Springfield who were watching the procession. They attacked the convention and drove them off. In the brawl both sides suffered many a bruise. Some of the convention were jailed and bound to appear before the Supreme Judicial Court.

Hence, that court became subject to obstruction. The farmers would not stand idly by and see their friends and fellow sufferers condemned by their legal equals and neighbors.

More conventions met in Hampshire County. Their one idea was to stop the lower courts so that debtors could not be harassed, and to stop the higher courts so that the people could not be tried for obstructing justice.

These conventions began sending their resolutions to other conventions in other counties. The delegates were now doing more than just listing their grievances. The gist of their resolutions was that the government of Massachusetts could not be worse and that it should be changed. But under the state constitution no change was possible until 1795.

Still the General Court kept rejecting the petitions of the county conventions on the grounds that they did not come from legalized assemblies.

New grievances arose. The peace treaty with Britain, signed on September 3, 1783, forbade Americans to trade with the British West Indies. Until the merchants got around this barrier to one of their greatest markets, a business slump made them all the more eager to collect in hard cash the money the farmers owed them.

In 1784 the General Court raised taxes again, but the taxes could not be collected in full. By the end of that year the state treasury was empty.

Pleading that his chronic gout prevented him from fulfilling his executive duties, John Hancock resigned as governor of the commonwealth in January, 1785. The real reason, however, was that he was frightened by the desperate economic condition, by the impatience of the creditors, and by the anger of the impoverished people.

After a bitter election campaign the popular votes for a new governor were so close that the election had to be decided by the legislature. On May 26, 1785, the reactionary Senate voted James Bowdoin,

[16]

General James Bowdoin.

the candidate of the conservative mercantile interests, into the governorship.

In the troubled circumstances, physically frail, scholarly James Bowdoin, who was suspected of Tory leanings, was not the best leader the commonwealth could have. His inaugural address made clear that he favored waiting for "an eventual cure" of the farmers' troubles, and for honoring the state's financial obligations. Rich James Bowdoin, the prosperous merchants' choice, was not popular with the poverty-stricken western farmers.

[17]

An artist's rendering of a scene typical of the conditions in Massachusetts that led to Shays' Rebellion. Here a blacksmith refuses to surrender his means of livelihood to a sheriff who has a legal writ to seize them in payment of the smith's debts.

In line with Bowdoin's statement of policy, the General Court voted to redeem at face value the certificates with which the veterans had been paid for their war service. A new tax was levied to raise sufficient revenue to accomplish this "principle of honor," as Bowdoin called it. To raise the cash to pay previous taxes, however, most of the western Massachusetts veterans had had to sell their certificates at a discount. Now they were to be taxed to enrich the eastern merchants who had bought the certificates cheap.

With the deflation of money, wholesale price index levels dropped from 225 in 1780 to 90 in 1786. In spite of good crops, the farmers' produce was of no more value to them than, as they themselves put it, the stones in their fields.

The county conventions urged the General Court to charter banks that would issue paper money and, by thus inflating the currency, cause a rise in prices. The farmers could see no difference between the government stamp on a piece of paper and actual coin. But the merchants could easily see the difference. They got the General Court to reject all petitions for an issue of paper money. Then the legislators adjourned in June, 1786, without offering the electorate any explanation of their refusal to help their constituents.

This whimsical behavior caused more and larger county conventions to gather. They kept in close correspondence with one another. The opposition to the government began to be unified. Once the conventions' resolutions for redress of the stupendous list of grievances got into circulation, they stirred up the riots that the conventions themselves self-consciously denounced. The conventions began to be associated with violence.

Captain Daniel Shays attended several of these conventions. He, too, was now in debt. In February, 1784, he had been called before the Court of Common Pleas by "yeoman" John Johnson for the enforcement of a promissory note for sixty dollars. Shays did not appear, and judgment and costs were recorded against him. At the conventions, however, he stated that he was opposed to violent action. It seemed to him inconsistent for a convention to authorize a riot and at the same time peacefully petition the legislature.

In West Springfield, Captain Luke Day was less moderate. Since protecting the courts in Northampton in 1782, he had spent two hot months in Northampton jail for debt before he broke out on August 29, 1785, and went home. That humiliating experience had quite changed his loyalties.

Like his ancestors, the old Puritans of Massachusetts Bay Colony, Day believed that God might speak directly to him through His word in the Bible. Luke discovered a passage in Ecclesiastes (4:1) that seemed directly intended for the times: "Behold the tears of such as were oppressed, and they had no comforter; and on the side of the oppressor there was power." He would be a comforter, and he would get some power on the side of the oppressed.

[19]

An early-nineteenth-century view of the courthouse (right) in Northampton, Massachusetts, built in 1737. Here Luke Day defied the judges on August 29, 1787. The building stood near the easterly corner of the present courthouse lot on the northeast corner of Main and King streets.

Captain Day spent many of his evenings at Stebbins' Tavern, where he found plenty of other men who, like himself, had borne all they could by the summer of 1786. They believed with him that Scripture justified their actions. Luke Day drilled them for action.

On August 29, 1786, the Courts of Common Pleas and of General Sessions were to sit in Northampton. Throughout Hampshire County, that date had been anticipated as a day of deliverance from the oppressor. Before daylight, Captain Luke Day had started his troop north from West Springfield.

Sheriff Elisha Porter watched them enter Northampton to the music of their fifes and drums, and found himself helpless. He had thought of calling out the militia to stop them and send them home. Now, as he looked over the faces of these four hundred invaders of

[20]

the neat, prosperous river town, he recognized many of his militiamen among them. By noon the number of swords and muskets and hickory clubs had increased to five hundred. More men kept drifting in from the nearby towns.

Sheepishly Sheriff Porter took his wand of authority in hand and went to Clark's Tavern, where the judges had been putting on their long gray wigs and their black gowns. He led them in solemn procession to the courthouse. Usually there were plenty of people out on a court day to watch the ceremony. This time, the sixteen hundred cautious citizens of Northampton had shuttered their shopwindows and were staying in their houses. They had no intention of getting their heads broken by interfering as the men of Springfield had done three years before.

Captain Luke Day's men, with bayonets affixed to their muskets, surrounded the approach to the courthouse. The land around it was full of the other contingents. On the courthouse steps stood Captain Day himself. In his hand was a petition which he gravely presented to the judges. It stated that it was "inconvenient" to the people for the courts to sit that day, and it "entreated" the honorable judges to adjourn until the petitions of the conventions might be granted by the General Court.

The drums rolled. The fifes squeaked. The armed men shouted a cheer for their leader.

With as much dignity as they could manage, the judges walked back to Clark's Tavern to consider Day's document. The more they did so, the clearer it became to them that they had no authority with which to deal with the situation.

As the warm August afternoon wore on, Sheriff Porter kept bringing the judges word that the number of armed farmers was growing. Finally he estimated them at fifteen hundred.

The judges observed the sheriff's lack of confidence, and admitted that they had been taken by surprise.

[21]

"Tell them," the judges instructed Porter, "that the courts are adjourned *sine die*."

Sheriff Porter translated the legal Latin. "The judges," he announced to the mob, "have not named a day on which they will hold court again."

The farmers made all kinds of puns on "day" and the name of the leader from West Springfield. One of them dryly remarked: "That don't say they won't hold court at *night*."

Some thought he had a point there. They stayed around the courthouse until after midnight. But the rest gladly walked home. Cows had to be milked, and pigs fed. They were satisfied that they had kept their cows and pigs out of the clutches of their creditors for a while anyway.

# The Spirit of '86

Governor James Bowdoin was dismayed by the news of the disorder in Northampton. On September 2, he proclaimed it a treasonable proceeding, and directed Attorney General Robert Treat Paine to seize the leaders of the Northampton mob and all future mobs. He also instructed the law officers of the counties to suppress any further mobs with the militia.

Bowdoin's exasperation led him into a legal error. Stopping the lower courts was merely a misdemeanor. Only interfering with the Supreme Judicial Court would be treason. Also, he failed to reckon with the fact that much of the militia of Hampshire County was on the side of the court-stoppers and that the loyalty of the militia anywhere else in the state was not to be trusted. The militia could hardly be expected to fire upon their neighbors and, perhaps, their own brothers. The militia was, as it had always been, very independent-minded.

The courts were to meet in Worcester, the county seat of Worcester County, on Tuesday, September 5. That morning, the fifteen

An early-nineteenth-century view of the courthouse in Worcester, Massachusetts, which the rebellious farmers captured and held in September and again in November, 1786.

The old Worcester Court House as it looks today. Considerably remodeled, and moved from its eighteenth-century location it is now a private residence.

hundred inhabitants of the community awoke to the sound of fifes and drums. Some three hundred strangers were in their streets.

The Worcester people could not have been much astonished. Perhaps they felt relieved. In Worcester jail were eighty-four prisoners for debt, whereas two years before there had been only seven. Nearly four thousand suits for debt had been brought in the county, which contained only about ten thousand adult males in a total population of around fifty thousand. The entire population of Massachusetts, which then included Maine, was only 379,000.

The invaders had come from Hubbardston under Captain Adam Wheeler; from Barre under Captain Moses Smith; from Princeton under Henry and Abraham Gale; and from other towns. Only about one hundred of them carried muskets; the rest had stout clubs.

Worcester County Sheriff William Greenleaf had a clear directive from the governor. When confronted by a mob, he was to collect the militia. If the mob did not respond to the sheriff's persuasion to disperse, he was to order the militia to fire. The militia were to obey him.

General Artemas Ward, chief justice of the Court of Common Pleas, whose home in Shrewsbury was only five miles from Worcester, knew of this directive. Probably he had advised Governor Bowdoin to issue it and to have the chief justice of Massachusetts, Theophilus Parsons, verify its legality. Inflexible Artemas Ward would have no such lack of authority as had restricted the judges in Northampton. He was used to authority, having been a colonel in the French and Indian War, and later the first commander in chief of the Continental Army.

At the usual time for opening court, paunchy General Ward led his co-judges to the courthouse, which they discovered was surrounded by insurgents. Before this unruly crowd paced a sentry who leveled his musket at the stately procession of the embodiments of law and order.

Artemas Ward recognized the sentry as a former soldier of his. "Recover arms!" the general ordered him.

[24]

The stern voice of his old commander so awed the sentinel that he immediately presented his bayoneted musket in salute to the judge.

Sullenly the crowd parted to make a path for the justices. They proceeded up to the courthouse steps. At the top stood a file of men with fixed bayonets behind Adam Wheeler, whose sword was drawn.

"Open the doors," Judge Ward directed the town crier.

Within were revealed a party of rebels, their muskets leveled to fire.

Artemas Ward advanced until the bayonets of the men on the steps were against his protruding stomach. "Who commands these people?" he demanded. No one responded. He repeated the question, adding: "By what authority and for what purpose have you come here in arms?" Still no reply. "Who is your leader?" Artemas Ward shouted a third time.

Captain Adam Wheeler finally ventured to answer him. "I am not the leader," he said, "but I can say why we've come. We want the distress of the country relieved. There shall no courts sit in judgment upon us until our grievances are redressed."

Artemas Ward remembered the success of the committee on which he had served in 1782. It had calmed the anger of the men of Hampshire County by patient listening, and had won them over.

"Let me hear your complaints," he said. "Then I shall satisfy you that they are without just foundation."

"Put that in writing," Captain Moses Smith answered.

"I will not," Artemas Ward declared. "I care nothing for your bayonets. You may plunge them into my heart. But while that heart beats, I will do my duty."

The steel blades moved closer.

"Remove your bayonets," Ward said calmly. "I shall prove to you that you have been deceived and deluded."

The resolute old soldier was having a disquieting effect upon the armed men. Moses Smith ordered the drums beaten in order to drown

[25]

out Artemas Ward's voice. The bayonets advanced until one ripped the judge's black silk gown. Artemas Ward did not move an inch. Slowly the bayonets retreated.

Judge Ward mounted the courthouse steps. Although he was no orator and was inclined to stumble over words, he proceeded to address the mob. For nearly two hours he described the weakness of their complaints, the futility of their cause, the dangers they were inviting for themselves and their families.

The men frequently interrupted him. At one pause in his sermon they loudly protested that they would stand their ground until they got satisfaction.

Artemas Ward turned to Adam Wheeler. "Let your troops disperse," he admonished the captain. "You are waging war, which is treason. Its end for you will be" — he paused for effect — "the gallows!"

Then, as rain started to fall, the chief justice of the Court of Common Pleas led his judges to Patch's Tavern — "the United States Arms" — in the square before the courthouse. There he opened his court, only to adjourn it to the following day.

By the next morning reinforcements had increased the number of men holding the courthouse to four hundred. Noisily and defiantly they paraded in the square, calling on the people of Worcester to join them.

Then a message arrived for the judges from the Athol town meeting, a legally constituted body. It humbly petitioned them to hear no cases for debt except with the consent of both parties. Artemas Ward saw that granting this request would get him out of his dilemma with dignity. He adjourned the Court of Common Pleas *sine die*, but the Court of General Sessions only until November 21.

The men of Middlesex County were even more ready for the courts than they had been for the British redcoats eleven years earlier. A convention of delegates from twenty-seven Middlesex towns was meeting in the county seat of Concord to petition the legislature for relief. In Groton town alone, one out of every four men was being sued for debt. Some had as many as four suits against them.

On Monday, September 11, the men of Groton swarmed into Concord, led by Job Shattuck, who had fought in the French and Indian War, and had given both time and money to the Revolution. He was not going home from Concord unsatisfied, even if he had to lay siege to the courts that were to meet there on September 12.

Shattuck's followers were driving wagons full of hay for them to lie on in case such a siege materialized, and they had sacks of provisions and plenty of rum. On the Concord green opposite the Middlesex County Courthouse they proceeded to build a camp for shelter.

Before nightfall they had been joined by some ninety men from Worcester County, led by Adam Wheeler. Later came a troop from Hampshire County. There were, in all, some three hundred men in the encampment.

Rain poured down that night. The kegs of rum were broached. There were harsh words and oaths among the several leaders, but soon these petty rivalries were forgotten, and the companies were united under Job Shattuck. The men stuck sprigs of hemlock in their hats. It was the emblem of Luke Day's men, and it was to become the badge of the insurrection.

On the following morning the rain of the New England nor'easter was still drenching the town, so delaying the arrivals of the judges that the court had no quorum until 1 P.M. By that time Job Shattuck had personally delivered an ultimatum of "the voice of the People of this county" that the court was not to sit until the government had redressed the people's grievances.

The convention in the Concord meetinghouse had announced that it intended to keep peace in the county, but it wanted just what Shattuck's men did, and it was afraid of the drunken men camped on the green. Sheriff Loammi Baldwin declared himself helpless against

[27]

The William Whiting house, Great Barrington, Massachusetts, where the rebels forced the judges to sign a pledge not to molest them.

these armed farmers, for most of his militia were among them.

When the judges sent for protection to the convention, a committee of delegates recommended that the judges not proceed to the courthouse. Fuming, the judges peered through the rain-streaked panes of Jones' Tavern, and concluded that the convention might be showing sound sense in advising them to stay warm and dry. To save face, the judges opened court in the tavern — and immediately adjourned it until November.

On the same September 12, the judges of Berkshire County arrived in Great Barrington, the county seat, to hold court. They were hopeful that they would find the people of this frontier region reasonable, for the resolutions of the county convention at Lenox in late August had been the most moderate of all. And the militia had been called out to protect the justices.

The judges' hopes fell, however, as soon as they saw the courthouse in the hands of some eight hundred farmers who had held it all the previous night. The farmers were calling on the militia in the courthouse square to stand by their own people. Within the ranks of the militia were loud arguments over loyalties.

Chief Justice William Whiting was much in sympathy with the farmers. He proposed that General John Paterson, who commanded the militia, divide his men into those opposing the sitting of the courts and those who approved. Presently only two hundred of the latter stayed with the general, who had been all too agreeable to Judge Whiting's suggestion. On the spot, the judges adjourned *sine die*.

The rebels were not satisfied with this easy victory. A committee followed the judges to William Whiting's house, where they demanded a signed agreement that the court would not sit until the legislature reconvened. Whiting signed gladly. With somewhat less cheerfulness, so did two of his colleagues. But old Jahleel Woodbridge, who had been a judge since before the Revolution, swore that he would resign his commission sooner than put his name to this bond with anarchy.

Satisfied now, the crowd broke open the jail and freed all the debtors in it. Sheriff Caleb Hyde was deliberately too occupied elsewhere to note the names of the leaders or their followers.

In Bristol County in the east, however, the loyal citizens of Taunton turned out three hundred strong on that same September 12 to support Major General David Cobb and his militia of four hundred, augmented by the Plymouth County militia. A band of farmers did come into town to stop the courts. But the courts, whose chief justice was the same David Cobb, adjourned *sine die*, and the farmers went home in good humor. Things were not so bad in Bristol County anyway.

The spirit of '86 had spread into New Hampshire too. On September 20, two hundred armed men surrounded the legislature in

[29]

Exeter, and proposed to besiege it until it granted their demands for an issue of paper money and a reduction in taxes.

General John Sullivan, who had fought through the Revolution, was serving the first of his three terms as governor of his native state. He had no fear of the bayonets pointed at him as he strode through the statehouse door and confronted the rebels. Bluntly he told them they were fools. He did not deny a rumor that a company of artillery was on its way to disperse them.

Neither side wanted bloodshed, the soldiers perhaps even less than the farmers. Who could continue to live in the tight community of a New England town after he had fired on his neighbor? The insurgents took to their heels. Governor Sullivan called out the state guard to make sure they did not stop running until they were back on their farms.

The spirit of '86 had also spread into Vermont. In August, two hundred distressed farmers had met in Rutland and proposed killing all lawyers and deputy sheriffs. Homespun Governor Thomas Chittenden told them that relief measures were only temporary cures for their troubles. "Be frugal," he lectured them. "Be diligent, practice agriculture, set your wives to spinning — and your troubles will soon end."

The Vermonters believed their beloved "One-eyed Tom." He, too, was a wily farmer. The disturbances calmed down.

There were similar events that year in New York, New Jersey, Pennsylvania, Maryland, Virginia, North Carolina, South Carolina, and Georgia. The Rhode Island legislature, however, had obliged its farmers by issuing paper money and forcing the merchants to accept it in payment of debts.

Asthmatic Governor James Bowdoin of Massachusetts had had no military experience, and he did not have the confidence of his people. He could only rely on the forms of law and order. Governor

[30]

Bowdoin called the General Court into an emergency session to commence on September 27.

So far, the battling farmers had made no attempt to stop the Supreme Judicial Court from sitting in any county. Their concern had not been for this high court for criminal cases. But when the Supreme Court met in Worcester on September 19, 1786, it indicted eleven leaders of the insurgents for having been, at Worcester a week earlier, "disorderly, riotous, and seditious persons."

The same court was to sit in Springfield on September 26. Doubtless it would indict the Hampshire County men for having obstructed the lower courts in Northampton four weeks previously.

The men of Hampshire County strongly believed that they had acted no more criminally than had the patriots of Lexington. Many, like Luke Day, had prayed for God's guidance, and it had been shown to them in Holy Scripture. It took them no time at all firmly to determine to resist the Supreme Court.

The incidents at Worcester and at Concord had shown these former soldiers that a leader was essential. It took them much time to decide who it should be. Adam Wheeler, possibly the best choice, was already under indictment. Job Shattuck had earlier paid a fine for leading a riot against the silver tax; they wanted a younger man anyway, and one whose record was blameless. Luke Day was a good speaker and a practical planner, but they distrusted his emotional way of being "inspired" by the Bible; such men could become dictators, and prove uncooperative with their fellows. The choices narrowed down until the men were desperate. Then someone thought of Captain Daniel Shays.

[31]

# The Rebellion Becomes Shays'

Shays was known from the conventions he had attended as compassionate but temperate, level-headed but fiery enough to take action when aroused. Everyone admired the Pelham militia he had drilled. His men in the Revolution had liked him; the men of Pelham liked him now. And his skirts were clean; he had not been with Luke Day or with any other party at Northampton, where Sheriff Porter had taken careful note of the insurgents' names.

A committee of Hampshire County farmers went to Conkey's Tavern in Pelham to inform Captain Shays that the choice of the people had fallen upon him.

Daniel Shays protested. The delegation persisted. The men of Pelham added their insistence; Shays would bring honor to their town. In a village like Pelham no individual has much choice of independent life or action. He must conform to the thinking of the community or be ostracized. Daniel Shays had had enough of ostracism in 1780. Otherwise he was no coward. Perhaps against his better judgment he consented. He would lead his fellows against oppression, and stop the court at Springfield, even though he knew that he would be committing treason.

That same year of 1786, the command of the Hampshire County militia had been given to Major General William Shepard of Westfield, who had won a captaincy in the French and Indian War, and had fought throughout the Revolution. Now the head of a family of nine, he was a deacon of the Congregational church, and he had sat in the lower house of the legislature for two years. He was unshakably on the side of government by law and order.

It was an easy matter for General Shepard to learn of the plans of the "Shaysites," as the rebellious farmers were now called. He saw the danger of their moving on Springfield, and he knew his duty. Not

*Above*, William Conkey's Tavern in the "hollow," Pelham, Massachusetts, from a photograph taken about 1900. In the eighteenth century such a tavern was a highly respectable meeting place for the men of a community — a kind of club. Daniel Shays, a close friend of Conkey's, used this tavern as his headquarters, and drilled his men before it. Along with the rest of the Prescott section of Pelham, the tavern was destroyed about 1930 in the construction of the Quabbin Reservoir. *Below*, The sign of William Conkey's Tavern, front (left) and back (right).

Major General William Shepard, from John Trumbull's painting of the Battle of Trenton, in the Yale University Art Gallery, New Haven, Connecticut.

only did he have to protect the court, but he had to defend the federal arsenal which had been established in Springfield in 1777.

General Shepard had so little military equipment at his disposal that he persuaded Secretary of War Henry Knox to give him the key to the arsenal. From it he took a small cannon and four hundred muskets. With the latter he armed the two hundred volunteers he called from the neighborhood to reinforce his two hundred militiamen. He planted the cannon before the Springfield courthouse, and surrounded it with his little army, which was soon increased to some nine hundred men.

On Tuesday morning, September 26, Daniel Shays rode down the two miles of Springfield's single street, lined with red and yellow houses. He was at the head of about seven hundred men, only a fourth of whom had any weapon but a club. When they saw Shepard's cannon, they hooted. "The government's puppy," they called it, knowing what a falsetto bark it had.

Respectfully Captain Shays saluted General Shepard, and asked permission for his men to parade. Shepard was too wise in the ways of old soldiers like the Shaysites to refuse. Many of the farmers were wearing their Continental Army uniforms.

As Shepard's men by the courthouse watched their former comrades marching, there were not a few who pulled the white paper strip — the badge of the government — from their own hat, and moved into Shays' orderly ranks. And throughout the morning men from other towns than Pelham drifted into Springfield to fall in behind their new leader.

The parade over, Shays called a council, whose consensus was that a petition to the judges be written. It stated that the farmers would withdraw on the judges' pledge that they would not be indicted for bearing arms. It pleaded that no cases be heard without the consent of both parties. It stipulated that the farmers not be taxed for the cost of the militia arrayed against them. They themselves were paying their own expenses and giving of their own time for the cause of real justice. Shays himself presented the petition to Chief Justice David Sewall.

On Wednesday, September 27, Judge Sewall and his colleagues respectfully replied in writing that they could not "do anything inconsistent with the important duties of their body."

When Shays' men learned of the judges' answer, they grew restless. They threatened to attack, even to kidnap the uncooperative judges. They paraded again.

The militia counterparaded. Those of the fifteen hundred Springfield citizens who ventured on the street that Wednesday afternoon prudently carried a sprig of hemlock in one pocket and a strip of white paper in another. The town was "very melancholy," wrote one diarist, and the houses were "rendered the scenes of female distress" as "brother was arrayed against brother, father against son."

[35]

The judges could not have done any business anyway, for they could not impanel a jury; all the veniremen were either guarding the courthouse or marching with Shays.

On Thursday morning, spies reported to Shepard that the Shaysites were determined to rush the courthouse. Shepard probably advised the judges to open court if they must, but to adjourn it immediately afterward, for he would have to move his forces to defend the arsenal, a mile and a half away. At any rate, the judges did open and adjourn.

Shepard withdrew to the arsenal on the hill, leaving the courthouse with its vacant courtroom for Shays and his men to occupy as a gesture. Both leaders had privately agreed to cooperate in order to avoid bloodshed. Both sides quietly withdrew at a signal the leaders had arranged.

# The Government Draws Its Sword

While Daniel Shays' men were parading in Springfield, Governor James Bowdoin was telling the General Court in Boston that what the rebels needed was punishment. He did not recommend any legislation that might relieve the cause of the troubles in the west.

The Senate passed a Riot Act. This provided punishments for armed gatherings which did not disperse within one hour after the sheriff had read the Riot Act to them. Their property was to be confiscated; they were to be given public whippings; they were to be imprisoned for one year, during which time they were to be whipped every three months. The Senate also suspended *habeas corpus*, a man's basic right in a free society to safeguard his person from illegal confinement.

The legislators of the lower chamber were more sympathetic to

[36]

the grievances of their constituents than the self-interested senators, but they had heard the governor's instructions. For a month the House of Representatives, which had to pass on the Senate's acts, debated a program of punishment, but reached no conclusion.

The farmers, however, knew that harsh measures were under consideration. A circular letter went out from Pelham to the town meetings throughout Berkshire and Hampshire counties, dated October 23, 1786. It called on the selectmen of the towns "to assemble your men together, to see that they are well armed and equipped . . . and ready to turn out at a minute's warning . . . properly organized with officers." The letter was signed "Daniel Shays," although Shays later denied that he had put his name to it.

Major General William Shepard lost no time in reporting this letter to Boston. He was desperately worried about protecting the Springfield arsenal.

The panic-stricken legislature immediately passed the Riot Act, suspended *habeas corpus*, and empowered the governor to call out the militia. Then it adjourned on November 18, having done only a very little to relieve the distress of the people.

Immediately a convention met in Worcester and declared the legislature misguided.

The Court of General Sessions was to meet in Worcester on November 21. On that day, the convention and a gathering of some 160 farmers confronted the judges, again led by Artemas Ward. The leaders of the insurgents were Adam Wheeler, Job Shattuck, and Henry Gale.

Artemas Ward resignedly let the unpopular Sheriff William Greenleaf read the Riot Act.

The rebel leaders interrupted the sheriff. They demanded redress of their grievances. One of the heaviest of these was Sheriff Greenleaf himself and the high fees he charged for executing judgments against debtors.

"If you consider my fees for criminal executions as oppressive," Sheriff Greenleaf retorted, "you need not wait long for redress, for I will hang every one of you, gentlemen, with the greatest pleasure and without charge."

While the sheriff was declaiming this threat, one of the rebels stole up behind him and stuck a sprig of hemlock in the back of his hat. This impudence was greeted with such jeers and cheers that the helpless judges retired. As the governor had instructed them to do, they opened court in Patch's Tavern, and immediately adjourned it.

A week later, the court was to meet in Cambridge in Middlesex County. Governor Bowdoin was determined that this court be fully protected.

Future president John Quincy Adams, then a senior at Harvard, wrote in his diary for November 27, 1786: "This evening just before prayers about forty horsemen arrived here, under the command of Judge Prescott, of Groton, in order to protect the court tomorrow from the rioters. We hear of nothing but Shays and Shattuck."

For, also from Groton, were coming Job Shattuck and Oliver Parker with about seventy irate followers. Parker and Shattuck quarreled over leadership, however, and the reinforcements they expected from Worcester and Bristol counties never showed up. Then these Middlesex men learned that the militia were after them with government warrants for their arrest. Hastily they scattered to their homes.

The rumor was correct. One hundred and sixty armed horsemen started combing the countryside for the leaders, including Adam Wheeler and Henry Gale, to apprehend them for their participation in the earlier defiance of the courts at Worcester.

Early on November 30, this troop reached Job Shattuck's house. Shattuck had fled to a friend's house two miles away, but a loyalist tipped the cavalry off to this refuge. When Shattuck saw the horsemen approaching, he ran, but he was tracked by his footprints in the snow to the bank of the Nashua River. There he grappled with one of his pursuers. Another slashed at Shattuck and cut the cartilage of his knee. The wounded Shattuck was carried in triumph to Boston and dumped into jail.

The government now had a prisoner, but unwisely it had created a martyr for the rebellious farmers. Strong, athletic Job Shattuck had not only been crippled, but he was being cruelly ill-used in jail. He had been transported away from his friends, and would be tried before a strange and hostile jury. There was a tremendous uproar from his followers. Reports spread that the government troops were damaging property and harming women and children.

The capture of Job Shattuck served to galvanize the loyalties of the insurgents to one another. Furthermore, every man of them now recognized that he had his own skin to save.

Two days after Shattuck's imprisonment, Daniel Shays sent out another circular letter — this time from Worcester, where he had called a meeting of local leaders.

"The seeds of war are now sown," Shays wrote. "I request you . . . and every man to supply men and provisions to relieve us with a reinforcement. . . . We are determined here to carry our point. Our cause is yours. Don't give yourselves a rest and let us die here, for we are all brethren."

Then, with Adam Wheeler, who had escaped capture, Shays began collecting stocks of ammunition from neighboring towns.

The governor knew that Shays would try to prevent the Court of Common Pleas from meeting in Worcester as it was scheduled to do on December 5. He was also afraid that thereafter Shays would lead his men, whom rumor had estimated at five thousand, into Boston to rescue Job Shattuck. Governor Bowdoin put Boston under military guard, and ordered the Worcester militia to protect the court.

On Sunday, December 3, Shays marched 350 men into Worcester and billeted them with the inhabitants of the town.

In spite of the governor's fear that the militia could not be trusted,

An early view of Main Street in Worcester.

170 of them turned out on Monday morning. They paraded down Worcester's Main Street to face the rebels at the courthouse. Captain Howe of the militia sent one of his officers to inquire by what authority his path was being blocked.

"Come and see for yourself!" was the answer the rebels sent him.

Captain Howe addressed his militia with spirit. He ordered them to fix bayonets and charge. Seeing them advance, the rebels panicked and fell back to the hill opposite the courthouse. The militia passed them and returned up Main Street, and were dismissed.

[40]

By Monday afternoon, the number of insurgents in Worcester had risen to about one thousand. About sunset snow began to fall, and during the night it blocked the roads. No more reinforcements could get through. The blizzard continued all through Tuesday, December 5.

By Wednesday the rebels were thoroughly cold and thoroughly famished. They were too poor to buy food or pay for shelter. Yet Shays managed to keep them orderly. He refused to let them take anything not offered them. But Shays did not have the force of personality to rally their spirits as George Washington had done with his similarly suffering soldiers at Valley Forge and Morristown. Everyone recognized that it was clearly impossible to march through the snow to Boston, especially with so few men, to oppose the soldiers in the capital.

Shays spent the day conferring with the delegates to the recent convention in Worcester and with the leaders of the rebels who had managed to get to Worcester before the snowfall. They decided to petition the legislature for the restoration of *habeas corpus*, the release of Shattuck from Boston jail, and complete pardon and safety for all who had taken arms. They had risen, the petition explained, because they could not provide for their wives and children or pay their debts; they had no desire to overthrow the commonwealth. They promised to be peaceful providing the petition was granted in its entirety.

There now was nothing for them to do but go home and wait for the government's answer. On Thursday morning they began plodding back through the snow, moving in companies for fear of being overtaken by pursuing cavalry. There were few who did not get frostbite. One of them fell in the snow and, unable to rise, froze to death.

An early-nineteenth-century view of the armory in Springfield, Massachusetts. Before it burned in 1824, it consisted of two red wooden storehouses, soldiers' barracks, a brick powder magazine, and one dwelling. The present Springfield Armory occupies the same site on State Street.

# The Arsenal at Springfield

Anxiously the government waited to see what Shays would do next. Their worry was increased by alarming reports from General Shepard concerning new local leaders in Berkshire County, especially Colonel Eli Parsons, and the men they were recruiting.

Daniel Shays kept his plans very secret. After the fiasco in Worcester he returned to Pelham, where he and the local leaders conferred on strategy. Should they march on Boston to liberate Job Shattuck? Should they seize the Springfield arsenal for the sake of its stores of ammunition? Which should come first?

One conclusion was inescapable. They needed more men, and tighter organization. By December 9 they had named a committee of seventeen, mostly former officers of the Continental Army, to raise companies in the towns of Hampshire County. The companies were then to be organized into six regiments under Shays' command.

General Shepard and Sheriff Porter had no clear knowledge of what the Shaysites were up to. It seemed incredible to Porter that the courts which were to meet in Springfield on December 26 would be obstructed. The trouble, he thought, had shifted eastward into Worcester County, which was fortunately beyond his jurisdiction.

Considerably to Sheriff Porter's astonishment on the morning of December 26, Daniel Shays appeared in Springfield. He was riding a white horse, leading a well-armed, well-drilled company of some three hundred men. Luke Day was with him.

They had put their names to a written petition which Shays respectfully handed to the judges an hour before they were to convene their courts. It requested them "not to open said court at this time nor do any kind of business whatever."

The judges complied, equally respectfully, in writing. There were no real hard feelings among these people who knew they had to live together then and in the future. Two of the judges went to dinner with Luke Day and Thomas Grover, the rebels' editorializer.

Daniel Shays did not join that dinner party. He was oppressed with confusing thoughts. He could not wholly justify taking up arms until the Worcester petition had been answered negatively by the General Court. As he dismissed his men, he told them he hoped he would not have to call them out again.

Two weeks later, Shays met Rufus Putnam, his old friend and former commander, on a road near Pelham. Putnam told him that it would be impossible for the government to grant the Worcester petition. He pleaded with the rebel leader to give up. If Shays did not, he would surely be defeated and hanged.

The warning of this shameful fate terrified proud Daniel Shays. When Putnam asked if he would accept a pardon, Shays replied: "Yes. In a moment."

Governor Bowdoin had been disgusted with the delays and indecision of the legislators during the previous fall. When news of the latest incident at Springfield reached him on January 1, 1787, he determined to act boldly. He ordered an army of forty-four hundred men raised from the militia of five counties. It was to rendezvous at Roxbury on January 19, and the men were to serve for thirty days thereafter.

Bowdoin appointed Major General Benjamin Lincoln, who was living in retirement in Hingham, to head this army. Lincoln had been a singularly unsuccessful officer during the Revolution, and had even been forced to surrender his army, but he enjoyed the friendship of George Washington and had been appointed Secretary of War by the Continental Congress. Lincoln went to the merchants' clubs in Boston to raise money for keeping his troops in the field for thirty days. For, since the legislature was not in session, no state funds could be voted for this purpose. One hundred and thirty merchants gladly contributed to the cause of destroying the pesky farmers. Governor Bowdoin himself gave $750.

At dawn on January 20, General Lincoln led his army on the two days' march to Worcester, where the courts were to meet on January 23.

News of these military preparations in the east was not long in reaching the leaders of the rebels in the west. On January 15, Shays had ordered the officers of his district to bring their men to Pelham with ten days' provisions on the same January 19 that Benjamin Lincoln was commissioned.

Nevertheless, Shays was still hoping that the Worcester petition would be granted and that conflict with the government's superior forces might be avoided. He did not know that the governor had flatly rejected the petition, or that he had been offered a pardon if he submitted.

The district leaders, however, were not so hopeful. They knew

Major General Benjamin Lincoln. An enormously heavy man, he limped from a wound he got at the Battle of Saratoga, and he had a disconcerting habit of dozing off in the middle of a conference.

they now had to fight and win, or be forced into the "unconditional submission to infamous punishment" of which Shays' directive had warned them. For their own defense they would have to take the Springfield arsenal.

In West Springfield, Luke Day had four hundred men under arms and was drilling them daily on the village green. "My boys," he told them, "you are going to fight for liberty. If you wish to know what liberty is, I will tell you. It is for every man to do what he pleases, to make other folk do as you please to have them, and to keep folks from serving the Devil."

[45]

Eli Parsons had started from Berkshire County with six hundred men to join Shays and Day at Springfield.

To protect the arsenal, General Shepard had occupied Springfield on January 18. As he kept hearing of the insurgents' plans, he grew frantic. He had only nine hundred men of dubious loyalty. He could get no money from Boston to provide rum for them, not to mention fuel and forage. Again he plundered the arsenal, the supplies of which were intended for the use of federal troops only. Nineteen hundred veteran Continental soldiers would soon be in Springfield under the command of Captain Daniel Shays.

By January 23, Shepard had only five days' provisions. Luke Day's troops cut him off from help on the west, and Eli Parsons' troops on the north. Desperately he entreated General Lincoln to send a flying column against Shays' rear.

Lincoln pressed on through the bitter cold to rescue Shepard. Learning of this action, Shays had no alternative to marching on the arsenal and seizing it before Lincoln got to Springfield.

On January 24, Shays sent a message to Luke Day, asking for cooperation in the attack on the arsenal he was scheduling for January 25. Day, however, wanted the entire credit for Shepard's expected surrender. He replied that he could not help until January 26.

The messenger carrying Day's response from West Springfield stopped at a Springfield tavern to warm himself. Some of the other patrons of the tavern were loyal to the government. Suspicious of this West Springfield man, they treated him to warming drinks until he fell asleep. Then they filched the message, and carried it to General Shepard. Afterward they locked up the stupefied messenger.

Shays had taken Luke Day's lack of response as agreement. On January 24, he and his men began to march on Springfield. They reached it about 4 P.M. the following day.

In spite of the cold, they were in high spirits, even when they saw Shepard's troops on the brow of Arsenal Hill, their cannon com-

[46]

manding the road. They themselves were indifferently armed, but were thoroughly equipped with a fiery vocabulary. Advancing to within 250 yards of the militia, they had no expectation that the cannon might be used against them.

Gloomy General Shepard was even more depressed than usual at the thought that he might have to order his men to fire on their old friends, neighbors, and former comrades-in-arms. He sent an aide to beg Shays to stop and to find out what Shays wanted.

Back came Shays' answer: "Barracks, and the stores of the arsenal."

Again Shepard sent a messenger, one of Shays' former fellow soldiers in the Revolution. He warned Shays that Shepard would fire.

"That is all we want," said Shays.

The messenger reminded Shays that he also was defending his country.

"Then we are on the same side," Shays said.

"But we shall be taking very different parts today."

Shays had lost the doubt and indecision he had shown in his interview with Rufus Putnam. Now he was in command of an army.

"The part I shall take," Shays punned, "is the hill on which the arsenal stands."

"In that case," said the messenger, "you will lodge tonight in heaven — or hell. I know not which, but I hope it may be the former."

Shays ordered his men to march toward the arsenal on the double.

When they were one hundred yards away, Shepard ordered his men to fire the cannon. They deliberately aimed the first two shots over the heads of their friends. Still Shays' column moved forward. A third shot went into its ranks. So did a fourth and a fifth.

"Murder!" roared Shays' men.

Then they broke and ran, yelling "Murder!" Shays could not rally them.

The government men picked up three corpses — Ezekiel Root

[47]

The green of Petersham, Massachusetts, near which General Benjamin Lincoln routed Shays' army on the morning of February 4, 1787. From an early-nineteenth-century woodcut.

and Ariel Webster, of Gill; and Jabez Spicer, of Leyden. They carried them, along with the severely wounded John Hunter, of Shelburne, into Olivet Church opposite the arsenal. There Hunter died on the following day. The dead bodies were removed to a stable where they froze stiff before they were called for by friends.

# Pursuit

After the late-afternoon slaughter on Arsenal Hill, Daniel Shays got his men under control about five miles east of Springfield, and led them to Ludlow, where they spent that night. They were horrified and they were frightened. Benjamin Lincoln's army was camping that night only ten miles east of them. By the morning of Saturday, January 27, two hundred of Shays' rebels had deserted.

Hastily Shays moved his remaining men north to Chicopee to join Eli Parsons' forces there and avoid being trapped between Shepard and Lincoln. From there he sent a message to Shepard, requesting the dead and wounded. Shepard replied that if Shays would only attack the arsenal again, he would be furnished with as many dead as he wished.

It was no longer necessary for Shepard to show pity and try to conciliate Shays and his followers. By noon on January 27, General Lincoln and his advance guard had arrived in Springfield.

In spite of the fatigue of his men, who had been continually on the march for a week of frigid weather, Lincoln lost no time in getting into action. Shepard fully expected a second attack on the arsenal from Shays' and Parsons' combined troops. Lincoln sent a detachment of infantry to keep Luke Day from joining his allies, and a troop of cavalry northward to catch Shays and Parsons.

At three thirty in the afternoon, four of Lincoln's regiments, with four fieldpieces, crossed the Connecticut River on the ice. Luke Day's guard at the western end of the ferry made a feeble resistance, then ran like foxes.

When this guard reached Day's headquarters at Stebbins' Tavern, their comrades stampeded and fled north via Southampton to Northampton, dropping their muskets and knapsacks and ammunition along the way.

Hearing of Day's retreat, Shays moved his men north via South Hadley. The first to arrive there descended on Butts' Tavern to eat, and cleaned the place out. While they were inside, three loyal government men crept into the horse shed and fired on them, killing one, and wounding another. There were also shots from the windows of Smith's Tavern across the road. When Shays himself reached South

The tablet in Benton Park on State Street (about 100 yards south of Oak Street), Springfield, Massachusetts, marking the site of Shays' attack on the arsenal.

Hadley, he got these snipers to surrender by threatening to burn the structures down upon them.

In revenge, Shays' men plundered several houses which the frightened inhabitants had abandoned, and looted two barrels of rum. They took nine men captive. Shays tried to restrain them, but their fear of capture — and the rum — had made them reckless and uncontrollable. Only with some difficulty did Shays get them over the hills to Amherst by eight o'clock that night. There he released the nine prisoners.

The next morning, Luke Day and his men joined Shays in Amherst, a town fiercely loyal to the cause of the rebels. Almost every man in it followed Shays when he left on the following morning, January 28, to fortify himself in Pelham, which he reached in the late afternoon.

General Lincoln himself and the bulk of his pursuing forces stopped at Hadley. On January 29, he sent a mission to Shays under a flag of truce, urging him to disband his "deluded followers." If Shays would agree, Lincoln promised to recommend mercy to the General Court for Shays' common soldiers. Nothing was said about clemency for the officers.

Shays consulted his staff. Then, politely, as one general to another in those latter days of chivalry, Shays replied to Lincoln that they were "unwilling to stain the land, which we in the late war, purchased at so dear a rate, with the blood of our brethren and neighbors," but that they would lay down their arms only on condition that everyone be pardoned and that Lincoln take his forces back to Boston until the General Court acted on the several petitions before it.

This written reply was delivered under a flag of truce to Lincoln on the following day. Lincoln responded that he had no authority to grant a general pardon.

On February 2, the rebels caught Lincoln's scouts reconnoitering their position. No one in Pelham felt safe. More and more of Shays' men deserted. Shays decided to move to Petersham, where he expected to find a more secure position and a greater supply of provisions. By taking his men farther away from their homes, he hoped to prevent further desertions.

On the morning of February 3, Shays sent Adam Wheeler to General Lincoln with a last entreaty to extend to the officers the pardon Lincoln had offered the privates. Lincoln correctly suspected Wheeler's mission to be a delaying tactic, and refused. The general's scouts reported troop movements in Pelham. But it was not until 6 P.M. on February 3 that Lincoln learned that the whole of Shays' army was on the march eastward to Petersham.

The rebels reached Petersham at the end of the cold afternoon of Saturday, February 3. Most of them had frostbitten ears, fingers, and toes. Shays led them to the northern end of the town, where they would be out of the freezing wind.

Lincoln ordered his army to get three days' provisions and prepare to advance at 8 P.M.

The weather in Hadley in the valley was fairly warm when they set out over the hills on the thirty-mile march via Shutesbury and New Salem to Petersham. But about 10 P.M. they encountered the bitter northwest wind. By the time they reached New Salem, about 2 A.M. on February 4, a violent snowstorm broke. The artillery was in front of the army, which stretched for five miles along the road. The wheels of the gun carriages were wider than the path, filling it with loose snow and making traveling hideously uncomfortable. The men could not rest. There was no shelter for miles around. They had to keep marching in order to survive.

At nine in the morning of February 4, Shays' men looked out from the warm houses in which they were enjoying Sunday breakfast to see General Lincoln's advance guard with two cannons coming along the narrow road into Petersham. The eighteen-inch-deep new fall of snow had drifted so as to protect the flanks of the army.

The rebels rushed out and formed several disorderly masses on

Petersham hill. General Lincoln insisted that the Riot Act be read to them. Instead of disbanding, the rebels advanced. The government soldiers were ordered to fire, but they aimed their muskets into the snow.

The rebels recognized that the cannon could easily mow them down faster than they could advance along the path to attack. They ran for their lives over the back road out of Petersham toward Athol. Shays ran with them.

Lincoln's soldiers chased the fugitives for about two miles, and captured 150 of them. Most of the prisoners were privates. Lincoln made them swear an oath of allegiance to the government, then sent them home. Those who lived far away were given sleighs and provisions. They left with tears of joy and thankfulness.

No blood had been spilled, but scarcely a man on Lincoln's terrible thirty-mile march through the blizzard escaped damage from exposure. Many later died of pneumonia.

# Raids and Reprieves

On the same February 4 that began with the rout at Petersham, the General Court met to declare that a state of rebellion existed in the Commonwealth of Massachusetts. As usual, the court was a little slow in facing realities.

The legislature promptly put a price on the heads of the rebel leaders — $750 for Shays, and $500 each for Luke Day, Adam Wheeler, and Eli Parsons. But, on February 16, due partly to General Lincoln's urging, it voted pardons to privates and noncommissioned officers, provided they gave up their arms, took the oath of allegiance, and stayed on their good behavior for three years. During that time they were not to serve as jurors, hold any office whatsoever, teach school, sell liquor, or vote for any civil or military officers.

The General Court was quite aware that this Disqualifying Act would prevent the rebels from getting by legislation what they were losing by insurrection. It served merely to keep rebellious spirits alive.

Daniel Shays had escaped from Petersham with about three hundred wretched stragglers. At Chesterfield, New Hampshire, on February 5, he voluntarily ended his command. Two days later he reached Westmoreland, Vermont. He was practically alone by then, and had no spirit for continuing the fight. But Luke Day, who followed Shays' course, flaunted his weapons in Marlboro, Vermont, and Adam Wheeler was active in New York.

Shays moved from town to town, seldom sleeping more than a single night in any one place. He had no wish to be caught and hanged. He crossed into New York, where he had a sister in White Creek, and there conferred with Adam Wheeler, probably as to who would lead any further movements. He went to Canada, but got no help there. His wife turned up in Bennington, Vermont, where she was closely watched by the detachment of soldiers General Lincoln had sent after the fugitives. By February 25, Shays was back in Vermont; on that day he was imprisoned in Bennington for a debt of $50 owed to a Vermont farmer.

The scene of resistance in Massachusetts shifted to ever-turbulent Berkshire County. On February 7, 1787, General Lincoln started his army into that frontier region on the border of New York, and established his headquarters at Pittsfield four days later. His arrival led to wholesale surrenders of rebels, who hastened to take the oath of allegiance to the government of the commonwealth. Then, as the term of enlistment of his men expired, Lincoln kept dismissing them until his army of occupation numbered only thirty by February 21.

That date was being impatiently awaited by rebel leaders who had skipped across the border into New York and safety. Since there was no federal union of the states at that time and no federal constitution — merely the loose Articles of Confederation — the governors of the various states were under no obligation of any sort to hand over men wanted by other states.

As early as February 13, Eli Parsons, in New Lebanon, New York, began to rally the rebels. But the insurgents had lost the bold spirit they had had under Shays' command, when the cry, "Hurrah for Shays!" went up wherever they appeared. Now revenge, not the establishment of social justice, motivated them. They were burning the barns and fences and woodlots, and mutilating the horses and cattle, of those who had opposed them.

And they delayed too long. It was not until February 26 that a band of 130 men, under Captain Perez Hamlin, set out from New Lebanon to Pittsfield. By then General Lincoln's forces had been increased by militiamen serving under a new term of enlistment.

Discovering this, the rebels changed their direction southward to Stockbridge, where they appeared on the morning of February 27. They stopped at a tavern and refreshed themselves liberally. Then they divided into groups to plunder the houses of citizens like Jahleel Woodbridge who had oppressed them. They took several prisoners — and a great deal of liquor.

Those rebels who were sober enough to move on marched the prisoners down the road to Great Barrington. There they released the debtors from the jail, and moved on southward toward Sheffield.

On the road between South Egremont and Sheffield they were met by eighty militiamen under Colonel John Ashley. In a six-minute engagement, thirty rebels, including Perez Hamlin, were wounded. Two rebels were killed, and two militiamen. About fifty rebels were taken prisoner. Their captors sent them north to Lenox's large jail in a mile-long string of sleighs to the accompaniment of much jeering from the bystanders, especially as they passed through Stockbridge.

A stone marker on the site of the skirmish near Sheffield reads: "Last battle of Shays' Rebellion was here, February 27, 1787."

Marker on the road between South Egremont and Sheffield, Massachusetts, commemorating the last battle of Shays' Rebellion.

Hamlin's raid induced the General Court to give General Lincoln authority to march his forces into any United States territory whatever for the purpose of catching the leaders of the rebellion and bringing them to justice. New York and all the New England states except Rhode Island then agreed to yield up their refugees.

Consequently the tumult in the west died down as the rebels scattered for fear of capture. Except for isolated reprisals, which kept occurring until June, 1787, the country waited quietly to see what would happen to the captured insurgents.

The election of April 1, 1787, turned Governor James Bowdoin out of office and, by an overwhelming majority, reinstated the more liberal and lenient John Hancock as governor. Three quarters of the

[56]

legislature went out with Bowdoin. The new General Court, which contained almost twice the number of representatives from western districts, was of a quite different tone from its predecessor.

Grimly the judges traveled about the counties throughout April, holding trials of rebels who had been captured and imprisoned on the charge of treason. There was little sympathy for the judges — and much for the accused. The judges bowed to the spirit of forgive and forget, and were lenient.

Seven hundred and ninety of the indicted were pardoned. A few were fined and condemned to imprisonment or to public penance, but only one of the latter sentences was carried out. Fourteen were convicted of treason and sentenced to hang.

On April 26, Bowdoin retired as governor. On April 30, his successor, John Hancock, pardoned eight of the condemned, leaving two to be hanged, as examples, in Berkshire and Hampshire counties, and one each in Worcester and Middlesex. All of these, however, were reprieved, some of them as they stood on the gallows with the noose around their neck.

Daniel Shays, Luke Day, and Eli Parsons, all of whom were still at large, were excluded from pardon. So was Adam Wheeler. He had been captured in White Creek, but a band of some forty "Yorkers" had rescued him. Perez Hamlin died of his wounds.

For the time being these leaders were ignored. Under Governor Hancock's direction, the General Court worked at binding up the wounds of the commonwealth. The Disqualifying Act was repealed. *Habeas corpus* was restored. Court costs were reduced. Imprisonment for debt was outlawed, providing the debtor swore that he could pay neither what he owed nor the cost of his board in jail. Taxes were lowered, and the merchants were required to pay a fair amount of them. Hancock accepted the desired reduction in the governor's salary which the richer Bowdoin had refused as unconstitutional.

On September 12, Hancock dismissed the last of the militia on

[57]

duty to prevent disorder in the western counties. Order had been restored. On June 13, 1788, pardon was granted to even the previously excluded leaders of Shays' Rebellion, including Daniel Shays himself.

Daniel Shays was then living in Sandgate, a district of Arlington, Vermont. He did not prosper. In 1792 he was again jailed for debt.

In Arlington Shays found an old comrade-in-arms from the Revolution named Jonathan Danforth, a lawyer, to whom he gave power of attorney on April 25, 1791. Four years later, Danforth was appointed a judge in the Court of Common Pleas for the newly organized Schoharie County, New York. He moved to Middleburg, New York. From there he sent for Shays, whose wife Abigail had died, and helped him locate in the hills near Livingstonville, where he could farm the rich soil of the region.

Shays stayed there for about fifteen years, then moved to Cayuga County, New York. A report of him during his residence there says that he had a "noble and commanding figure, fine martial appearance, and was pleased with the title of General by which he was usually saluted."

In Cayuga County, Shays met young Jonathan Weston, who had been teaching school in Sparta (now part of Conesus) in Livingston County, New York. He returned with Weston to Sparta, and settled as a squatter on government land near the hamlet of Hungerford's in 1814.

Fourteen-year-old Millard Fillmore was then working in a wool-carding mill and living with Benjamin Hungerford, Shays' neighbor. Later Fillmore wrote of Daniel Shays, whom age must have withered:

> I remember Shays as a rather short, stout, unattractive man, and was always puzzled to understand how a man of such unattractive demeanor and so apparently retiring had ever been such a leader of men. I frequently enjoyed his hospitality, and, although thrown into company with much

Daniel Shays' home in Schoharie County, New York. The man in the photograph is unidentified.

older men, Capt. Shays always showed me every attention, and in their presence predicted an illustrious future for me. In latter years I remember that he drank rather heavily, but never associated with low companions, and prided himself on setting an excellent table.

Daniel Shays was an astute judge of character. In 1850, Millard Fillmore became the thirteenth president of the United States.
Another acquaintance of that time, William Scott, remembered Shays as "by no means commanding in person, his dress quite ordinary,

and there was nothing to mark him as one to take the lead. We wondered how the talkative old gentleman had become so prominent."

On April 1, 1815, Shays married forty-seven-year-old Rhoda Havens, widow of Darling Havens, one of Sparta's settlers and its tavern keeper. Shays moved to her farm, one mile east of Scottsburg. On April 23, 1818, he applied for a pension as a Revolutionary War officer, and was granted one in 1820. He was then worth only $40.62 in personal effects.

Daniel Shays died on September 29, 1825. He was buried in Union Cemetery in Conesus, a mile from his home. Only a simple slate, incised with a penknife "Da. Shays," marked his grave for many years. Now a blue granite stone stands above it, reading: "Daniel Shays — Revolutionary War — 1747-1825."

# The Rewards of Rebellion

While the condemned rebels of Massachusetts were awaiting what the General Court called "condign punishment," delegates from all the thirteen states except Rhode Island met in Philadelphia "in order to form a more perfect union, establish justice, ensure domestic tranquillity."

More than any other single factor, the lack of justice and of domestic tranquillity evidenced by Shays' Rebellion caused the Continental Congress to call that convention. The insurrection had separated Massachusetts into a debtor class and a creditor class. The creditors throughout the country were now determined to guard their property against further attack. Men of property knew all too well that rebellion is a dangerously contagious disease. The uprising in Massachusetts proved to them that a strong central government was necessary to protect their interests. It would be definitely constituted to "suppress insurrections" (Constitution of the United States, Article I, Section 8).

Many of the delegates to the convention were like the self-made merchant Elbridge Gerry of Massachusetts who had no intention of letting the political control of the nation slip from the grasp of the propertied class. Other delegates, although men of property also, were more experienced than the provincial New Englanders. They were not so afraid of the people. Virginia's George Mason said in answer to Elbridge Gerry: "We ought to attend to the rights of every class of the people . . . provide no less carefully for the . . . happiness of the lowest than of the highest order of citizens."

The miraculous result of the delegates' five months of labor to construct a good government was the Constitution of the United States. John Quincy Adams would say that it had been "extorted from the grinding necessity of a reluctant nation," and that "Shays' Rebellion was the extorting agency." Historian Charles Francis Adams would write that Shays' Rebellion was "an episode second in importance to none . . . one of the chief impelling and contributory causes to the framing and adoption of the Constitution."

The people of Massachusetts, farmers and merchants alike, could see that the republican form of government the Constitution guaranteed to every state promised protection for all classes. In spite of some querulous opposition from the diehard westerners, they were among the first to ratify the Constitution and to swear to abide by its provisions.

It was now up to the people themselves to elect responsible representatives to implement the Constitution for the benefit of all. Benjamin Lincoln had pointed out in his protest against the Disqualifying Act of February 16, 1787, that "the good people of the state" must "exert themselves in the appointment of proper characters in the executive and legislative branches of government."

Theoretically, in a democracy an insurrection like Shays' Rebellion is never permissible. But at the time it occurred, the characters in the executive and legislative branches of government in Massachusetts had small regard for actual conditions and for different points of view. Both the rebellious farmers and the conservative, self-protecting merchants were too inexperienced in the meaning of democracy to trust one another. Even though the government of Massachusetts remained for a time in the hands of the rich merchants, nevertheless, thanks to Shays' Rebellion, those merchants saw that a greater tolerance on their part for the interests of the farmers meant greater prosperity for all.

Daniel Shays himself lived to see that tolerance become nationwide. America had fought another war with Britain, and it had brought the political downfall of the self-interested New England merchants. The American hero of that War of 1812, Andrew Jackson, sat in the White House. Jacksonian democracy, of which the Shaysites were the first examples, brought into at least intellectual practice the principles of the Declaration of Independence which Shays had fought to maintain.

The lessons of democracy are as hard to learn as its responsibilities are heavy to bear. The basic issue is how rich and poor are to live together with equal privileges. The issue was not solved by Shays' Rebellion, which first raised it in the infant American nation, nor by Pennsylvania's similar Whiskey Rebellion of 1794. It flowered in the insurrections of the Populist movements of the 1870's, where the conflict was again over the rights of farmers and the demand for paper money. The issue did not begin to find a peaceful solution until the spirit of Franklin D. Roosevelt's New Deal measures in the 1930's for the relief of the oppressed and the economically distressed became a part of the American conscience.

A hemlock-shaded tablet to the right of the meetinghouse in Pelham, on the Daniel Shays Highway (Massachusetts Route 202), commemorates Daniel Shays' attempts to oppose "unjust laws." Americans have reason to be grateful to him.

# BIBLIOGRAPHY

## I. *Books*

Barber, John Warner. *Historical Collections*. Worcester: Warren Lazell, 1844.

Coolidge, Mabel Cook. *The History of Petersham, Massachusetts*. Petersham: Petersham Historical Society, Inc., 1948.

Davis, Andrew MacFarland. *The Shays' Rebellion, a Political Aftermath*. Worcester: American Antiquarian Society, 1911.

Doty, Lockwood Lyon. *A History of Livingston County, New York*. Geneseo: Edward E. Doty, 1876.

Green, Mason A. *Springfield, 1636-1886*. Springfield: C. A. Nichols & Co., 1888.

Holland, Josiah Gilbert. *History of Western Massachusetts*. Springfield: Samuel Bowles and Co., 1855.

Lincoln, William. *History of Worcester, Massachusetts*. Worcester: Charles Hersey, 1862.

Lockwood, John H. *Westfield and Its Historic Influence*. Westfield, 1922.

Martyn, Charles. *Life of Artemas Ward*. New York: Artemas Ward, 1921.

Minot, George Richards. *The History of the Insurrections in Massachusetts*. Worcester: Isaiah Thomas, 1788.

Parmenter, C. O. *History of Pelham, Massachusetts, from 1738 to 1898*. Amherst: Carpenter & Morehouse, 1898.

Smith, Joseph E. A. *The History of Pittsfield*. Springfield: C. W. Bryan & Co., 1876.

Starkey, Marion Lena. *A Little Rebellion*. New York: Alfred A. Knopf, 1955.

Taylor, Robert J. *Western Massachusetts in the Revolution*. Providence: Brown University Press, 1954.

Trumbull, James Russell. *History of Northampton, Massachusetts*. Northampton: Gazette Printing Co., 1902.

Warren, Joseph P. *The Shays' Rebellion*. Unpublished thesis in the Harvard College Library, Cambridge, Mass.

## II. *Articles*

Booth, Henry A. "Springfield during the Revolution." In *Papers and Proceedings of the Connecticut Valley Historical Society*, Vol. II, October 21, 1903. Springfield, 1904.

Farnsworth, Albert Shaw. "Shays' Rebellion." In *Massachusetts Law Quarterly*, Vol. XII, No. 5, February, 1927.

Green, Samuel A. "Groton during Shays' Rebellion." In *Proceedings of the Massachusetts Historical Society*, Vol. I, 2nd Series, 1884-85. Boston, 1885.

Gregg, Arthur B. "The Lost Years of Daniel Shays." In *Schoharie County Historical Review*, Vol. 18, No. 2, October, 1954.

Hansen, Millard. "The Significance of Shays' Rebellion." In *The South Atlantic Quarterly*, Vol. 39, No. 3, July, 1940.

Holland, Park. "Reminiscences of Shays' Rebellion," edited by H. G. Mitchell. In *The New England Magazine*, Vol. XXIII, No. 5, January, 1901.

Moody, Robert E. "Samuel Ely: Forerunner of Shays." In *The New England Quarterly*, Vol. V, January, 1932. New York: Ams Reprint Co., 1963.

Noble, John. "A Few Notes on Shays' Rebellion." In *Proceedings of The American Antiquarian Society*, Vol. 15. Worcester, 1902.

Riley, Stephen T. "Dr. William Whiting and Shays' Rebellion." In *Proceedings of The American Antiquarian Society*, Vol. 66, Part 2, October, 1956. Worcester, 1956.

Shriner, Charles A. "Shays' Rebellion." In *Americana*, Vol. XX, April, 1926.

Smith, Jonathan. "Features of Shays' Rebellion." In *Proceedings of the Clinton, Massachusetts, Historical Society*, 1905. Reprinted in *The William and Mary Quarterly*, Third Series, Vol. V, No. 1, January, 1948.

Smith, William L. "Springfield in the Insurrection of 1786." In *Papers and Proceedings of the Connecticut Valley Historical Society*, Vol. I, October 1, 1877. Springfield, 1881.

Wade, Herbert T. "The Essex Regiment in Shays' Rebellion." In *Essex Institute Historical Collections*, Vol. 90, No. 4, October, 1954.

Wood, F. J. "Paper Money and Shays' Rebellion." In *Stone & Webster Journal*, Vol. 26, May and June, 1920.

Marker on the Daniel Shays Highway opposite the Pelham Town Hall at the junction of Amherst Road and Massachusetts Route 202.

# Index

[65]